FlashRevise Pocketbook

AQA  nology

Philip Allan Updates, an imprint of Hodder Education, an Hachette UK company, Market Place, Deddington, Oxfordshire OX15 0SE

Orders

Bookpoint Ltd, 130 Milton Park, Abingdon, Oxfordshire OX14 4SB
tel: 01235 827827   fax: 01235 400401   e-mail: education@bookpoint.co.uk

Lines are open 9.00 a.m.–5.00 p.m., Monday to Saturday, with a 24-hour message answering service. You can also order through our website: www.philipallan.co.uk

© Philip Allan Updates 2010
ISBN 978-1-4441-1541-3

First published in 2006 as *Flashrevise Cards*

Impression number   5   4   3   2
Year   2015   2014   2013   2012   2011

Printed in India

Hachette UK's policy is to use papers that are natural, renewable and recyclable products and made from wood grown in sustainable forests. The logging and manufacturing processes are expected to conform to the environmental regulations of the country of origin.

P01942

102738

Stress

53 General adaptation syndrome (GAS)
54 Autonomic nervous system (ANS)
55 Hypothalamic–pituitary–adrenal system
56 Sympathomedullary pathway
57 Immune system
58 Type A personality
59 Social readjustment rating scale (SRRS)
60 Daily hassles
61 Workplace stress
62 Hardiness
63 Emotion-focused coping
64 Problem-focused coping
65 Anxiolytic drugs
66 Biofeedback
67 Cognitive behavioural approach

Social influence

68 Conformity
69 Normative influence
70 Internalisation
71 Social roles
72 Protection from harm
73 Obedience
74 Foot-in-the-door technique
75 Agentic state
76 Authoritarian personality
77 Cost–benefit analysis
78 Independent behaviour
79 Locus of control
80 Individualist culture

Psychopathology (abnormality)

81 Deviation from social norms
82 Failure to function adequately
83 Biological (medical) model
84 Neurotransmitters
85 Hormones
86 Psychodynamic model
87 Defence mechanisms
88 Psychic conflict
89 Classical conditioning
90 Operant conditioning
91 Social learning theory (SLT)
92 Biological preparedness
93 Cognitive model
94 The diathesis–stress model
95 Chemotherapy
96 Antipsychotics (major tranquillisers)
97 Electroconvulsive therapy (ECT)
98 Psychoanalysis
99 Systematic desensitisation
100 Cognitive behavioural therapy (CBT)

The multi-store model (MSM)

Q1 Identify three ways in which the sensory memory, STM and LTM stores differ.

Q2 In this model, what moves information from sensory memory to STM?

Q3 What is this model's main limitation regarding LTM?

Q4 The MSM claims that information must flow through STM to reach LTM. What suggests this is not always the case?

ANSWERS

A1 Encoding; capacity; duration.

A2 Attention.

A3 It does not discriminate between different kinds of LTM: semantic, episodic and procedural.

A4 • In Shallice's study of the effects on memory of a motorcycle accident, KF could encode new long-term memories, even though his STM was severely impaired.

• Flashbulb memory, where information seems to go straight into LTM.

***examiner's* note** This model, although open to various criticisms, has provided a useful framework for research into memory.

(1) ANSWERS

Short-term memory (STM)

Q1 What is the capacity of STM?

Q2 How can this capacity be increased?

Q3 What is the Brown–Peterson technique for measuring the duration of STM?

Q4 In Shallice's case study of KF, which part of KF's STM was damaged, and which was relatively unaffected?

ANSWERS ▶▶

A1 7 ± 2 pieces of information.

A2 Chunking, i.e. putting small pieces of information together into one 'chunk'.

A3 People are asked to remember a trigram (a set of three consonants) and recall it after varying periods of time, after having completed an interference task of counting aloud backwards.

A4 Auditory — damaged; visual — relatively intact.

***examiner's* note** The MSM gave some basic information about the nature of STM, but more detail is provided by the working memory (WM) model.

Long-term memory (LTM)

Q1 According to the MSM, what moves information from STM into LTM?

Q2 Which kind of LTM appears to be the most resistant to damage? Give an example of research suggesting this.

Q3 After a fall skiing, Dr S did not recognise his friends. He skied down the mountain and correctly diagnosed himself. (a) Which part of his LTM was damaged? (b) What evidence is there here that the other two parts of LTM were unaffected?

ANSWERS ⟫

A1 Rehearsal, and specifically elaborative rehearsal, i.e. processing by meaning.

A2 Procedural memory. In the study of HM, and a similar study of Clive Wearing, episodic and semantic memory were severely damaged, but procedural memory was not.

A3 (a) His episodic memory. (b) His ability to continue skiing shows that procedural memory was not affected, nor was his semantic memory, since he was able to make an accurate self-diagnosis.

***examiner's* note** LTM is a blanket term, referring to memories which last anywhere from 30 seconds to a lifetime. Some researchers have specifically investigated VLTM (very-long-term memory), e.g. the Bahrick et al. study of memory for faces.

(3) **ANSWERS**

Rehearsal

Q1 What is the effect of rehearsing material?

Q2 Which kind of rehearsal helps to keep information in STM for brief periods of time?

Q3 Define elaborative rehearsal.

Q4 How can rehearsal be used to explain (a) the primacy effect and (b) the recency effect?

ANSWERS

processing information to establish or prolong a memory

A1 Strengthens the memory trace and therefore makes recall more likely.

A2 Maintenance rehearsal.

A3 Processing material in terms of its meaning.

A4 (a) The first items in a list can be rehearsed before they are followed by too many other items, moving them into LTM (elaborative rehearsal).

(b) The final items in a list can be rehearsed before recall, since no further items follow, keeping them in STM (maintenance rehearsal).

***examiner's* note** Because rehearsal is such an effective way of improving recall, some studies of memory use an interference task to prevent it being used, e.g. Peterson & Peterson's study of the duration of STM.

 **4** **ANSWERS**

Encoding

Q1 According to the MSM, what is the main way in which information is encoded in STM?

Q2 Identify a study that supports this idea.

Q3 (a) What is semantic encoding? (b) In which of the stores in the MSM is it used?

Q4 How would (a) directions on a map and (b) music be encoded in LTM?

ANSWERS

A1 Acoustically.

A2 Conrad's participants showed acoustic confusion when recalling letters from STM, e.g. 'M' for 'N', even though the letters were presented visually; Baddeley's study into encoding in STM also showed acoustic confusion in recall from STM.

A3 (a) Encoding by meaning. (b) In the LTM.

A4 (a) Visually; (b) acoustically.

examiner's note Overloading a system is a useful technique in psychological research. What goes wrong can be very informative, e.g. Conrad's study, asking participants to recall more than was easily manageable from STM. The acoustic confusion they showed provided information about encoding in STM.

 **ANSWERS**

The primacy and recency effects

Q1 What is (a) the primacy effect and (b) the recency effect?

Q2 What is the effect on recall when participants are asked to count backwards between learning material and recall?

Q3 How do the primacy and recency effects support the MSM?

Q4 How can these effects be related to interference?

ANSWERS

A1 (a) The first few items on a list are well remembered, compared with those in the middle.

(b) The last few items on a list are well remembered, compared with those in the middle.

A2 The recency effect disappears.

A3 Primacy: suggests the first few items have been processed into LTM.

Recency: suggests the last few items are still in STM.

A4 There is more interference from other items for middle items than for early or late items, since several items come before and after them.

examiner's note Ebbinghaus's early memory research demonstrated the primacy and recency effects — a robust finding, which has been replicated many times.

Declarative memory

Q1 Which parts of LTM make up declarative memory?

Q2 Does declarative memory link to explicit memory (i.e. relying on conscious remembering) or implicit memory?

Q3 When Clive Wearing's LTM was damaged, he (a) could no longer recognise his old college, (b) could not remember who wrote *Romeo and Juliet* and (c) when shown pictures of the Queen, mistook her for a friend. Which parts of declarative memory were affected in each example?

ANSWERS

A1 Episodic and semantic memory.

A2 Explicit memory depends largely on the declarative knowledge system; implicit memory depends on the procedural knowledge system.

A3 (a) Episodic memory; (b) semantic memory; (c) confusion between episodic and semantic memory.

***examiner's* note** Research suggests that declarative memory is less robust than procedural memory, so it may not always be appropriate when talking about memory to refer to LTM in general.

 **7** **ANSWERS**

Working memory (WM)

Q1 Identify three functions of the central executive.

Q2 Why is this model known as 'working' memory?

Q3 You need to remember an unfamiliar phone number. Which part of WM is used to remember the area code? Which part is used when you repeat the rest of the number to yourself?

Q4 Which parts of WM are involved when buying a round of drinks — repeating the orders on the way to the bar and remembering where each friend is sitting?

ANSWERS

Baddeley & Hitch: model of STM emphasising memory as an active process

A1 Processes information from any of the senses; allocates attentional resources to an appropriate slave system; holds small amounts of information while other information is being processed.

A2 'Working' emphasises that it is an active system, rather than the more passive short-term system (MSM).

A3 The central executive holds the area code, and the articulatory loop rehearses the rest of the number.

A4 Repeating the orders uses the articulatory loop, and remembering where people are sitting uses the visuospatial sketchpad.

***examiner's* note** The emphasis on active processing is an advance on the MSM, but the model is limited by looking only at STM.

 **ANSWERS**

Flashbulb memory

Q1 Why is this kind of memory called a 'flashbulb' memory?

Q2 Identify two features that Brown & Kulik claim characterise flashbulb memories?

Q3 What six features of a flashbulb memory did Brown & Kulik find people usually recalled?

Q4 How does the phenomenon of flashbulb memory challenge the MSM?

ANSWERS

A1 Because the memories referred to by this term are sharp and detailed, as though lit up by a strong light, as in flash photography.

A2 They are accurate; long-lasting; vivid; emotional

A3 Where they were; what they were doing; who told them; how they felt; how others felt; the aftermath of the event.

A4 Flashbulb memories appear to go straight into LTM without the rehearsal specified in the MSM.

examiner's note Since they are by definition significant events, flashbulb memories may be well remembered because they are often discussed (and therefore rehearsed).

(9) ANSWERS

Schema

Q1 How are schemata developed?

Q2 What practical use do schemata serve?

Q3 A schema held about a group of people is a s.......................... .

Q4 How could the idea of schemata explain Allport & Postman's findings when people were questioned about a picture of a white man attacking a black man, but remembered the black man as the attacker?

ANSWERS

A1 They are built up on the basis of past experience.

A2 They reduce the amount of information processing needed.

A3 stereotype

A4 Presumably what they remembered was influenced by a stereotype (schema) of black men as being more likely to be criminal and/or violent.

***examiner's* note** Because they are based on past experience, schemata can be useful in reducing processing effort when we come across new information. However, they can sometimes lead to distortion.

Reconstructive memory

Q1 What was the name of the story which Bartlett used to demonstrate reconstruction?

Q2 Why did he choose a Native American folk story?

Q3 What did Bartlett mean by 'effort after meaning'?

Q4 What kind of distortion did he refer to as 'flattening'?

ANSWERS

Bartlett: remembering is an active process, built from the elements of stored experience

A1 'War of the Ghosts'.

A2 So that it would be unfamiliar to his participants and, therefore, a good test of how we deal with new material.

A3 We try to make sense of our experiences in terms of what we already know.

A4 Forgetting unfamiliar details.

***examiner's* note** Bartlett's studies stimulated a lot of research into the reconstructive nature of memory. This has been important ultimately in the area of EWT, with the practical aim of finding ways to encourage accurate recall.

Eyewitness testimony (EWT)

Q1 Who has been the leading researcher in this area?

Q2 What is the major criticism of much of her research in this area, and why?

Q3 The effect on EWT of introducing inaccurate information when witnesses are questioned is known as the m......................... effect.

Q4 Yuille and Cutshall carried out a study on the effect of stress on EWT in witnesses of an armed robbery. Identify *one* positive aspect of this study, and *one* problem with it.

ANSWERS

A1 Loftus.

A2 Low ecological validity, as she used filmed material.

A3 misinformation

A4 It had high ecological validity, as it investigated EWT of a genuine crime; the researchers had no control over aspects of the event such as the nearness of witnesses to the crime, so could not assess the effects of these aspects of the experience.

***examiner's* note** There has been a great deal of research interest in EWT as it is an important influence on jurors and the verdicts they return. It is therefore important that it is as accurate as possible.

Leading question

Q1 Loftus & Zanni asked participants 'Did you see the (or a) broken headlight?' Which is a leading question, and how would it affect memory?

Q2 In the Loftus & Palmer study of a car crash, which aspect of the question influenced participants' estimate of speed?

Q3 What evidence was there that the question continued to distort participants' memory of the crash a week later?

ANSWERS

a question put in such a way as to suggest an answer

A1 The word 'the' suggests that there was a broken headlight to be seen, and therefore is a leading question, influencing participants to confirm that there was a broken headlight.

A2 Whether they heard the word 'smashed' or 'hit' etc. when asked to estimate the car's speed.

A3 Those who heard the word 'smashed' were more likely to remember having seen (non-existent) broken glass.

***examiner's* note** Research has demonstrated that the way in which questions are asked is a strong influence on EWT. This has led to more refined questioning techniques, e.g. those used in the cognitive interview, to improve accuracy.

Detail salience

Q1 What is 'detail salience'?

Q2 In Loftus's 'weapon focus' study, what was remembered less well by participants who saw the 'gun' scenario?

Q3 Identify a study where participants were not misled by questions about something central to the scene they witnessed.

Q4 In Loftus's study of a simulated armed robbery, why was the violent version of the video less well remembered?

ANSWERS

A1 One or more aspects of what is witnessed are seen as of particular importance, so less attention is given to other aspects.

A2 What the man looked like, as they were less able to identify him from a set of photos.

A3 Loftus's purse study. The purse was salient to the theft scenario, so participants were not misled about its colour.

A4 Violence interfered with the processing of information, leading to poorer recall.

***examiner's* note** There are many factors which can interfere with memory at all three stages: registration; storage; and retrieval. Detail salience and violence are registration factors, which affect the initial processing of information.

Cognitive interview

Q1 Why is hypnosis seldom used to try to get more information from witnesses?

Q2 Why are witnesses asked to reinstate mentally the external context of the witnessed event, and their own internal context, i.e. thoughts and feelings at the time?

Q3 Witnesses are asked to recall an event in a variety of orders and from a variety of perspectives. To which theory of memory does this relate, and how?

Q4 Identify *three* aspects of the enhanced cognitive interview.

ANSWERS

a technique based on memory theory used to question witnesses of crimes

A1 It is unreliable, as people under hypnosis are very suggestible to the interviewer's ideas.

A2 This information may provide cues that trigger additional useful information.

A3 The spreading activation model of memory. It is hoped that the variety of orders and perspectives may trigger relevant linked information.

A4 Minimising distractions; getting the eyewitness to speak slowly; adjusting the way questions are asked to suit the individual; reducing anxiety; avoiding judgemental or personal comments.

examiner's note The cognitive interview has been shown to be highly effective. It is used widely and is an example of a useful application of psychological theory.

 ANSWERS

Memory strategies

Q1 Ways of improving memory are called m.................... techniques.

Q2 Processing by meaning has been shown to be important in remembering information. This is called s.................... processing.

Q3 Two ways in which we organise material to improve memory are c.................... clustering and h.................... organisation.

Q4 Identify *two* aspects of imagery which increase its effectiveness in enhancing recall.

ANSWERS

A1 mnemonic

A2 semantic

A3 categorical; hierarchical

A4 Bizarreness; interactive imagery.

examiner's note Improving memory is an important application of psychological theory, e.g. in revising for exams and improving EWT. The importance of meaning, the organisation of material to be remembered, and visual imagery have all been the focus of research in this area.

Attachment

Q1 (a) What do Schaffer & Emerson call the first stage of attachment formation? (b) How long does it last?

Q2 At about what age do infants start to form a strong attachment to one individual?

Q3 How does the 'cupboard love' theory explain attachment?

Q4 (a) Give two examples of social releasers.
(b) What is their effect?

ANSWERS

A1 (a) Asocial or indiscriminate stage. (b) Up to about 6 weeks.

A2 From about 7 months.

A3 Attachment develops to the caregiver associated with providing food.

A4 (a) Smiling; crying; clinging. (b) We are thought to be innately programmed to respond to these kinds of behaviour, which trigger a care-giving response.

***examiner's* note** Bowlby developed a stage theory of attachment similar to that of Schaffer & Emerson. It gives more detail about characteristic behaviour of infants during the formation of their major attachment. It adds a further phase, starting at around the age of 2, where the infant's conscious awareness allows further development of the relationship with the attachment figure.

Secondary drive hypothesis

Q1 What is the basic principle used by this hypothesis to explain how attachments are formed?

Q2 What is a primary drive?

Q3 According to this hypothesis, what motivates a child to form an attachment with the caregiver?

Q4 How does the study by Harlow & Zimmerman, in which monkeys were raised in isolation, challenge this hypothesis?

ANSWERS

Dollard: attachment is a learned response associated with a primary drive

A1 Attachment is a learned response.

A2 An innate need, e.g. for food or shelter.

A3 An association is formed between satisfaction of the primary drive (food) and closeness to the caregiver, so this closeness (attachment) becomes a secondary drive.

A4 The monkeys preferred the terry cloth surrogate to the wire surrogate that provided milk, suggesting that contact comfort is more important than food.

***examiner's* note** Food does not seem to be the central factor in the formation of attachment. Many infants form their main attachment with someone who does not feed them regularly.

Strange Situation

Q1 Which three key observations are made using this technique?

Q2 What is the main ethical concern raised by the technique?

Q3 How might a child's regular experience of daycare affect their behaviour and therefore the attachment category they are placed in?

Q4 The technique is usually carried out with the child and the mother. Why might this not always be appropriate?

ANSWERS

Ainsworth: technique to test the quality of attachment between infant and caregiver

A1 The child's response to *separation*; how the child interacts with the *stranger*; the child's response to reunion with the mother.

A2 Causing the child distress, especially as this is a lengthy procedure (seven episodes of 3 minutes each).

A3 The child could show little distress at separation, and little emotional response at reunion, because these are both regularly experienced. The child could then be incorrectly classified as anxious–avoidant.

A4 Schaffer & Emerson found that many children form their main attachment to their father or a sibling, so measuring the quality of attachment to the mother may not be appropriate.

***examiner's* note** The Strange Situation is a technique developed in one culture and applied to another, where it might not be a valid measure.

 ANSWERS

Anxious–avoidant

Q1 In a British or US sample, what is the typical percentage of children classified as anxious–avoidant in the Strange Situation?

Q2 How does the anxious–avoidant child respond when separated from the caregiver?

Q3 How does the child respond when reunited with the caregiver?

Q4 How does the child respond when left alone with a stranger?

ANSWERS

A1 20%.

A2 The child does not seem particularly bothered.

A3 There is no very strong response. The child may avoid contact with the caregiver.

A4 The stranger and caregiver are treated in similar ways.

***examiner's* note** The classification of anxious–avoidant indicates that the child is insecurely attached to the caregiver. However, this behaviour could merely reflect the child's experience, e.g. of often being left and then collected from daycare. For this child, the Strange Situation would not be so strange.

Anxious–ambivalent (or anxious–resistant)

Q1 In a British or US sample, what is the typical percentage of children classified as anxious–ambivalent in the Strange Situation?

Q2 How does the anxious–ambivalent child respond when separated from the caregiver?

Q3 How does the child respond when reunited with the caregiver?

Q4 How does the child respond when left alone with a stranger?

ANSWERS

A1 10%.

A2 The child typically becomes extremely distressed.

A3 The child is angry, and tries to avoid contact, but this is combined with attempts to be close to the caregiver.

A4 The child is distressed and cannot be comforted by the stranger.

***examiner's* note** Ainsworth proposed that caregiver insensitivity is linked to both anxious–avoidant and anxious–ambivalent characteristics. The caregiver of an anxious–avoidant child may reject or may, on the other hand, try to force interaction with an unwilling infant. The caregiver of an anxious–ambivalent child may misunderstand the child and behave inconsistently.

Separation anxiety

Q1 What is separation anxiety, and what is it believed to show?

Q2 Kagan et al. carried out a cross-cultural study of separation anxiety. What did they find?

Q3 Which other kind of anxiety appears at roughly the same time as separation anxiety?

Q4 What are the three stages of a child's response to extended separation from the caregiver?

ANSWERS

A1 Anxiety shown by an infant when separated from the main caregiver, assumed to show that an attachment has been formed.

A2 They found a similar pattern across very different cultures, in terms of the age when separation anxiety started to be shown, when it reached a peak, and when it started to subside.

A3 Stranger anxiety.

A4 Protest; despair; detachment — the PDD model.

***examiner's* note** The finding that separation anxiety peaks at roughly the same time across very different cultures suggests that its development is universal. It is therefore likely to be innate and the result of maturation.

Cross-cultural studies

Q1 Why are cross-cultural studies carried out?

Q2 How might the relatively high proportion of anxious–avoidant German infants in several cross-cultural studies be explained?

Q3 What did van Ijzendoorn & Kroonenberg find when they compared the variation between and within cultures?

Q4 What problem does this suggest there might be in making cross-cultural comparisons?

ANSWERS

studies comparing two or more cultures

A1 They help to establish the extent to which characteristics are innate, and the extent to which they are shaped by the individual's culture.

A2 Characteristics found desirable in German children, i.e. non-clingy and relatively independent early on, are reinforced behaviours.

A3 The variation within cultures was 1½ times as large as the variation between cultures.

A4 Conclusions about cultures can only be general. More detailed conclusions would need to take into account sub-cultural and individual differences.

examiner's note Cross-cultural studies have been used to establish the relative influences of nature and nurture on development. More recently, a transactional model has studied how these factors interact in particular cultures.

 ANSWERS

Imprinting

Q1 What is meant by a 'critical period'?

Q2 What did Bowlby believe was the critical period for infants to develop an attachment?

Q3 The concept of a critical period has been replaced by that of a sensitive period. What is the difference between the two?

Q4 Klaus & Kennell drew a parallel between attachment and imprinting. What did they suggest led to this bond?

ANSWERS

A1 A fixed period in which a behaviour must develop, e.g. the following response in goslings soon after hatching. Once developed, it is irreversible.

A2 From 6 months up to about 3 years.

A3 The latter is more flexible. There is a period when a behaviour is most likely to develop, but it can develop outside this period.

A4 Hormones present around the time of birth make both the mother and infant sensitive to bond formation.

***examiner's* note** Imprinting is a reflex, while attachment involves emotions, so drawing a parallel may not be appropriate. Bowlby's critical period of up to 3 years old has been challenged, e.g. by Kadushin, who found that many children adopted at over 5 years old were still able to form attachments.

Evolutionary perspective

Q1 In evolutionary terms, what purpose would seeking proximity to the caregiver serve for an infant?

Q2 What name is given to the innate characteristics and behaviour patterns of the infant which elicit care-giving and ultimately promote survival?

Q3 How does the infant balance safety and exploration?

Q4 Give one piece of evidence for cross-cultural similarity in attachment.

ANSWERS

behaviour can be explained in terms of how it is adaptive, i.e. promotes survival and reproduction

A1 It would promote protection and safety.

A2 Social releasers.

A3 Using the caregiver as a secure base.

A4 Kagan et al. showed that separation anxiety developed, peaked and started to subside at much the same time across a range of cultures.

***examiner's* note** Evolutionary theory, which influenced Bowlby's attachment theory, accounts well for the characteristics of attachment. Many competing theories relate attachment to food, although research such as Harlow & Zimmerman's study of monkeys has shown that food does not seem to be crucial in the formation of attachment.

Internal working model (IWM)

Q1 The IWM is a schema, i.e. a c........................ r........................ of relationships.

Q2 What kind of IWM is developed by anxious–ambivalent/ resistant infants?

Q3 The IWM predicts a correlation between early attachment and later relationships. Name one supporting study.

Q4 An alternative view is that our ability to form relationships depends on innate characteristics, i.e. t........................ .

ANSWERS

in Bowlby's attachment theory, a template for future relationships

A1 cognitive representation

A2 The IWM that relationships are unpredictable, since caregivers of infants in this category tend to be inconsistent in the way they interact with them.

A3 Hazan & Shaver (link with romantic relationships); Main & Cassidy (link with behaviour and attitudes of children aged 3–6); Main & Goldwyn (link with quality of attachment to own child).

A4 temperament

***examiner's* note** Some studies have found a link between patterns of attachment in infancy and the nature of relationships in later life, but this can often be explained in other ways. It has been suggested that children who are appealing to their parents will also appeal to others, and so are likely to have good relationships both with parents and with others.

Maternal deprivation hypothesis (MDH)

Q1 Which three kinds of development did Bowlby suggest would be affected if a child was separated from the main caregiver?

Q2 Bowlby claimed that these effects would be irreversible. Give one piece of evidence suggesting that this is not necessarily true.

Q3 Did Rutter consider privation or disruption more likely to have an adverse effect on children's development?

ANSWERS

Bowlby: separation from major caregiver causes child irreversible cognitive, emotional and social damage

A1 Cognitive, emotional and social.

A2 Suomi & Harlow (caretaker monkeys); Kadushin (late adoptions); Koluchova (Czech twins); Freud & Dann (concentration camp children).

A3 Privation.

***examiner's* note** While some aspects of the MDH have been modified, it has nonetheless had a huge positive influence. It has changed attitudes to the care of infants, and changed the ways in which children are cared for in hospitals, institutions, daycare and at home.

Affectionless psychopathy

Q1 What is the main characteristic of affectionless psychopathy?

Q2 In his study of 44 juvenile thieves, how could the fact that Bowlby both made the diagnosis of affectionless psychopathy and drew the conclusions be seen as problematic?

Q3 This problem could have been overcome by using a double-blind technique. What does this involve?

ANSWERS

A1 Emotional maladjustment, in which the individual shows no guilt or remorse for his or her behaviour.

A2 His diagnosis might have been influenced by his expectations, as he also knew which children had been separated from their mothers when younger.

A3 Data are collected by someone who is unaware of the hypothesis, e.g. diagnosis by a psychiatrist aware of the criteria for affectionless psychopathy but not which boys had experienced separation from their mothers.

examiner's note Bowlby believed separation from the major caregiver would have an adverse effect on emotional development (affectionless psychopathy), as well as social and cognitive development.

Longitudinal study

Q1 What is the main advantage of this kind of study in relation to investigating attachment?

Q2 Participants may drop out of a longitudinal study, so the sample becomes smaller. Why may this be a problem?

Q3 Give one of the main findings of the Hodges and Tizard study of institutionalisation when they compared children at 16.

Q4 Give one of the main conclusions drawn by Rutter et al. in their longitudinal study of Romanian orphans.

ANSWERS

a study in which data are collected about participants over a period of time, usually years

A1 Long-term effects, e.g. of maternal separation, can be studied.

A2 Possible sample bias. Certain types of participants may be more likely to drop out than others, making the sample unrepresentative.

A3 Adopted children had better relationships at home than those restored to their natural parents. Both groups had social and emotional difficulties at school.

A4 There is considerable variation in the effect on children of institutionalisation; the psychological effects of profound privation in an institution can be substantially reversed as a result of placement with a good adoptive family.

***examiner's* note** Longitudinal studies are useful when examining the effects of early experiences on development. However, as they take place over a considerable period of time, they are expensive and participant drop-out limits the conclusions that can be drawn.

 **(29) ANSWERS**

Privation

Q1 In the context of child development, how is 'privation' defined?

Q2 How does it differ from 'deprivation'?

Q3 What were the outcomes of the studies of both the Czech twins and Genie?

Q4 Give *two* reasons which might account for these differences.

ANSWERS

the lack of any opportunity to form an attachment

A1 The child has no opportunity to form an attachment with a caregiver.

A2 Deprivation: not having a close attachment to a caregiver. Privation is only one reason for deprivation. Disruption is another.

A3 Czech twins: good recovery and essentially normal by age 14. Genie: poor recovery, little language acquired and limited social skills.

A4 Age: Czech twins discovered at 7; Genie at 13. Treatment: Czech twins lovingly fostered; Genie moved from foster family to families where she was ill-treated. Relationship: Czech twins formed a relationship with each other; Genie entirely alone until discovered.

examiner's **note** Bowlby makes no distinction between reasons why the child has no firm attachment. Rutter claims privation is more likely to have adverse effects than disruption.

Daycare

Q1 Why did Bowlby consider daycare inappropriate?

Q2 For which kinds of children did Pennebaker et al. find daycare had a poor outcome?

Q3 Identify *two* factors which have been shown to influence whether care by a childminder is a positive or negative experience for a child.

Q4 Using the Strange Situation technique, Belsky found that children experiencing more than 20 hours a week of daycare were more likely to be insecurely attached than those experiencing fewer than 20 hours. How might this study be criticised?

ANSWERS

any kind of regular childcare carried out by someone other than the main caregiver

A1 He believed that any separation would weaken the maternal bond, and so lead to an insecurely attached child.

A2 Shy and unsociable children, who found it threatening.

A3 The experience of the childminder; his/her willingness to stimulate the children; his/her willingness to form a bond with them; the child's temperament.

A4 The Strange Situation technique does not take into account the child's previous experience of being left with someone other than the primary caregiver; there may be a confounding variable between the groups compared, such as differences between mothers who use extensive daycare and those who do not.

***examiner's* note** Daycare may be beneficial for both child and mother, and for their relationship. Boulton found that many mothers who had given up work suffered from depression and loss of identity. Schaffer believed that a child will develop better with a mother who is happy at work than with one who is bored as a full-time carer.

Daycare:
social development

Q1 Identify *two* factors which might explain higher levels of aggression shown by children in daycare.

Q2 Identify *two* factors which might explain lower levels of aggression shown by children in daycare.

Q3 The quality of care appears to be a major factor in whether daycare has a positive or a negative effect on children's development. Give three examples of aspects of good-quality daycare.

Q4 Identify *one* additional factor that research has shown to influence whether daycare is likely to have a positive or negative influence on children's development.

ANSWERS

the social effects of daycare, for example on levels of aggression and relationships with other children

A1 There are more opportunities for aggression; they may learn from other children to resolve disputes in this way; aggression may be a way of getting attention from carers.

A2 They may learn early on the need to share toys and equipment; they may learn ways of dealing with disputes that are more positive than aggression; daycare may remove the child for periods of time from the aggression demonstrated by high-risk families.

A3 Physical setting; child-to-carer ratio; carer qualifications; activities geared to the needs of children; appropriate play materials; good relationships between carers and parents.

A4 The child's temperament; family background; gender.

***examiner's* note** While early research on daycare tended to focus on the possibility of it weakening attachment, recently there has been a shift in emphasis to its effect on children's social development and in particular aggression. This is important because early aggression has been found to be a major risk factor in later antisocial behaviour.

Experiment

Q1 Which two factors define a study as an experiment?

Q2 Which kind of experiment is carried out (a) in a setting controlled by the experimenter and (b) in a natural situation?

Q3 What kind of experiment is a study comparing the preferences in hobbies of extraverts and introverts? Why?

Q4 A study compares children's reading levels before and after a reading scheme is used. What kind of experiment is this?

ANSWERS

A1 The experimenter manipulates the IV across conditions to observe the effect on the DV. Participants are randomly allocated to conditions (in an independent groups design) or to the order in which conditions are carried out (in a repeated measures design).

A2 (a) Laboratory; (b) field.

A3 A quasi-experiment. It is comparing pre-existing groups, as participants cannot be randomly allocated to extraversion or introversion conditions.

A4 A natural experiment. It takes advantage of a naturally occurring event (introduction of the reading scheme) not controlled by the researcher.

***examiner's* note** Quasi- and natural experiments do not meet the criteria of an experiment. A genuine experiment is replicable and demonstrates cause and effect, as long as confounding variables are adequately controlled.

Variables

Q1 A study investigating efficiency compares worker productivity at a toy factory from 9 to 10 a.m. (morning shift) and 7 to 8 p.m. (evening shift). (a) What is the IV? (b) What is the DV?

Q2 Confounding variables can be differences between participants in the conditions, i.e. s.................... variables, or differences in the testing situation, i.e. s............................ variables.

Q3 Identify *two* possible confounding variables in the study in Q1.

ANSWERS »

A1 (a) Time of day, i.e. what is different between the two conditions.
   (b) Number of toys produced, i.e. what is measured.

A2 subject; situation

A3 Different kinds of workers on the two shifts, e.g. in terms of training and experience; different toys might be produced by the two different shifts; only one of the 2 hours observed could contain a toilet or meal break; different supervisors could affect work rates.

***examiner's* note** Independent and dependent variables need to be operationalised, i.e. defined in terms of how they are to be used in a particular study.

Experimental design

Q1 What is a repeated measures design?

Q2 How is a matched participants design carried out?

Q3 Give one reason why this design is not often used.

Q4 A design with different participants in each condition is an i................................. g................. design.

ANSWERS ▶▶

A1 The same participants provide data in both or all conditions.

A2 Different participants provide data in each condition, each matched for important variables with participants in the other condition(s).

A3 It is time-consuming to match participants; an important characteristic may be overlooked in the matching process; if one participant drops out, the matched participant(s) must also be discarded.

A4 independent groups

***examiner's* note** A repeated measures design has the advantage of eliminating the effect of individual differences, since the same participants provide data in each condition, but raises problems of order effects and demand characteristics. An independent groups design eliminates order effects and reduces demand characteristics, but individual differences may affect the results.

Correlational analysis

Q1 What is a study using correlational analysis aiming to find?

Q2 In correlational analysis, there is no IV and no DV; instead there are two c.....-................................ .

Q3 How are the results of a correlational analysis usually shown graphically?

Q4 What does a correlation of 0.85 between the two variables being measured show?

ANSWERS

A1 Whether there is any association between two variables, i.e. that they tend to vary together.

A2 co-variables

A3 Using a scattergraph (scattergram).

A4 This shows a strong, positive correlation. High scores on one variable tend to be associated with high scores on the other variable.

***examiner's* note** Correlational analysis can show the strength and direction of an association between two variables. It cannot show cause and effect, or non-linear relationships, e.g. the curvilinear relationship between arousal and performance.

Naturalistic observation

Q1 Why might a researcher choose to use this method?

Q2 What is the main ethical issue with using it?

Q3 What is the main practical issue with using it?

Q4 In which type of observation does the researcher join in as part of the group being observed?

ANSWERS

observing behaviour in its natural setting with no attempt at manipulation

A1 It provides data on natural behaviour in a natural setting, so has high ecological validity. It is an effective way of studying children and animals.

A2 Invasion of privacy. People are observed without their knowledge or consent.

A3 Lack of control. Since the observation is taking place in a natural setting, the researcher has no control over what is being observed, which may therefore not run as planned.

A4 Participant observation.

***examiner's* note** This method produces rich data, high in ecological validity, but it is difficult to control or replicate the observations. Bias is possible in the data analysis, as the data are often qualitative and can only be analysed subjectively. This may be dealt with by using two observers, to establish inter-observer reliability.

 **37 ANSWERS**

Questionnaire

Q1 What is the difference between a questionnaire and an interview?

Q2 What is a closed-ended question?

Q3 Give one advantage of using a closed-ended question in questionnaires.

Q4 What are open-ended questions? Give one advantage and one disadvantage of using this kind of question in questionnaires.

ANSWERS

A1 Interviews are carried out face-to-face; questionnaires do not need to be.

A2 It provides the respondent with possible answers from which they must choose the one most applicable to themselves.

A3 The range of responses is limited, so analysis is straightforward. Comparisons between respondents are made easily.

A4 Respondents can answer the question in any way they wish. Advantage: no constraints on responses, so more likely to be accurate. Disadvantage: analysis is more complicated.

***examiner's* note** Questionnaires are efficient when collecting large amounts of data, particularly since they do not require the researcher's presence. However, people who return questionnaires may differ significantly from those who do not, so the data may be unrepresentative. The response rate is likely to be low.

Interview

Q1 Give one advantage and one disadvantage of unstructured interviews.

Q2 Which kind of interview includes some set questions, but also allows points of interest to be followed up flexibly?

Q3 Give one disadvantage of interviews compared with questionnaires.

ANSWERS))

A1 Advantage: the respondent can take the interview in whichever direction feels most appropriate. Disadvantage: the interview can easily go off track.

A2 Semi-structured.

A3 Because the interviewer needs to be present while the data are collected, an interview is more time-consuming than using a questionnaire, and fewer data are likely to be collected.

examiner's note The kind of interview chosen depends on the aims of the study. A structured interview is likely to provide data which are easy to analyse, and replication should be straightforward. On the other hand, it is likely that the richness of the data produced from a semi-structured or unstructured interview will be lost.

(39) ANSWERS

Case study

Q1 Give an example of a case study in psychological research.

Q2 A major problem with case studies is generalisability. What does this mean and why is it a problem?

Q3 Identify and explain one other problem with this method.

ANSWERS))

an in-depth study of an individual or small group of individuals who share a characteristic in which the researcher is interested

A1 Freud's studies of patients; Genie or the Czech twins (see Topic 30); HM's amnesia (see Topic 3).

A2 Applying conclusions drawn on the basis of a study to others who are similar to the participants. It would be unwise to assume that conclusions drawn from a study of only one or very few individuals would apply more widely.

A3 Researcher bias, where the researcher may interpret findings in line with his or her expectations; lack of accuracy of the information provided by the individual(s) may distort the findings.

***examiner's* note** This method has the advantage of providing rich, detailed data, but has limitations, such as issues of generalisability. However, for some topics, such as the effects of certain types of brain damage on human functioning, it is the best or only option available.

Hypothesis

Q1 Give another term for 'experimental hypothesis'.

Q2 What is a hypothesis predicting there will be no difference between conditions, or no relationship between variables?

Q3 What is the difference between a one-tailed (directional) hypothesis and a two-tailed (non-directional) hypothesis?

Q4 'Extraverts will prefer brighter colours than introverts.' Is this a directional or a non-directional hypothesis? Why?

ANSWERS

A1 Alternative hypothesis.

A2 Null hypothesis.

A3 Both predict that there will be a difference between conditions (or a relationship between variables), but a one-tailed hypothesis also predicts the direction of the difference or relationship.

A4 Directional — it states not only that there will be a difference between extraverts and introverts, but also which group will prefer brighter colours.

***examiner's* note** For most psychological research, the written report includes a research hypothesis. This is usually developed on the basis of psychological theory or previous research. Some research, which gathers qualitative data, may start instead with a more general research question.

Pilot study

Q1 In a memory experiment, a pilot study suggested that the use of the chosen materials could lead to a ceiling effect. What does this mean, and why is it a problem?

Q2 In a similar experiment, the pilot study suggested that the use of the chosen materials could lead to a floor effect. What does this mean, and why is it a problem?

Q3 A psychologist is planning a study using naturalistic observation of people offering help to pick up groceries. Identify *one* factor that may need adjusting as a result of her pilot study.

Q4 A study is planned using questionnaire data. Identify *one* aspect of the questionnaire that may need amending as the result of a pilot study.

ANSWERS ▶▶

A1 Most participants are likely to remember all or nearly all of the material they are asked to recall. The results will therefore not discriminate among participants and conditions.

A2 Most participants are likely to remember very little, if anything, of the material they are asked to recall, so again the results will not discriminate among participants and conditions.

A3 The place where the observation takes place, i.e. there are enough participants, but not so many as to make data recording difficult; the best place for observers to position themselves.

A4 Its length; the clarity of some of the questions.

examiner's note It is important to carry out a pilot study to identify potential problems before embarking on large-scale data collection, e.g. the appropriateness of materials and the clarity of instructions, so that necessary adjustments can be made. Feedback from participants in pilot studies can be useful in suggesting how the study could be adapted.

Ethics

Q1 Why is ethics of particular importance in psychology?

Q2 Who has produced guidelines in the UK to help researchers consider the ethical implications of studies they are planning?

Q3 Identify one ethical issue, other than deception, raised by Asch's conformity studies. How was this shown?

Q4 Why is deception sometimes necessary in research studies?

ANSWERS

a consideration of what is thought to be acceptable behaviour

A1 Psychological studies involve people (or animals) capable of a wide range of negative experiences, e.g. stress, humiliation. Every effort must be made to avoid such negative experiences during the study.

A2 The British Psychological Society (BPS).

A3 Footage of the study provided clear evidence that participants were stressed, e.g. sweating and tremors.

A4 Some studies would be compromised if participants were given full information. They could guess the aims of the study and perhaps change their behaviour; deception is necessary for the study to be viable.

***examiner's* note** Ethical concerns about studies, such as Milgram's, led to the development of more comprehensive guidelines. Psychological research carried out in universities now has to be approved by an ethics committee.

Informed consent

Q1 What is informed consent?

Q2 Why is informed consent considered necessary?

Q3 Who would be unable to give informed consent?

Q4 In these cases, what would the procedure be if the study were to be carried out?

ANSWERS

participants in a study should be given enough information to decide whether they wish to take part

A1 People should be given full information about the study and how the findings will be used, so that they can decide whether to take part.

A2 Participants giving their time to help with research should be treated with care and respect.

A3 Children; people with learning difficulties/mental health problems.

A4 Consent can be given on their behalf by a responsible person, e.g. a parent or guardian. As far as possible, the individual should also be asked for their consent.

examiner's note Fully informed consent is not always possible. In some cases, e.g. social influence research, giving full information would compromise the study and invalidate it. Here, a full debriefing is necessary when the study has been completed, and participants should be given the option of withdrawing their data.

Qualitative data

Q1 What is the difference between quantitative and qualitative data?

Q2 Even though qualitative research does not involve quantitative analysis, it often makes use of c......................, e.g. the percentage of children showing each kind of attachment behaviour in the Strange Situation.

Q3 A researcher interested in eating disorders aims to interview a number of participants and see which themes emerge in what they have to say. This is known as t...................... a...................... .

Q4 A major criticism of qualitative research is that it depends on i..................., and so may be affected by researcher bias.

ANSWERS

A1 Quantitative data are the result of measurement; qualitative data are descriptive.

A2 categorisation

A3 thematic analysis

A4 interpretation

examiner's note In practice, a lot of research studies collect both quantitative and qualitative data. In this way, the objectivity of quantitative data and the stringency of statistical analysis are combined with the richness and detail of qualitative data.

Reliability

Q1 Reliability is a measure of the c.............................. of a test or technique.

Q2 Which method is used to measure the reliability of a test over time?

Q3 Which method is used to measure the internal reliability of a test, i.e. whether it is testing the same thing throughout?

Q4 Which statistical technique is used to measure reliability?

ANSWERS

A1 consistency

A2 Test-retest reliability.

A3 Split-half reliability.

A4 Correlational analysis.

***examiner's* note** Reliability is important since a measuring tool which does not provide consistent measurements is of little use.

Internal validity

Q1 Internal validity is also known as e.................................... validity.

Q2 What is meant by internal validity?

Q3 Are field experiments more likely to be high or low in internal validity?

Q4 Give one reason why participants in Milgram's obedience study might not have accepted the experimental situation as presented.

ANSWERS))

A1 experimental

A2 The extent to which the outcome of a study is genuinely the product of the procedures of the study.

A3 Low, since there is little control in field experiments.

A4 The participants might have wondered why they were needed, as the shocks could have been given by the experimenter; they might not have believed that such extreme shocks were genuine.

***examiner's* note** The internal validity of a study can be compromised by a range of factors, e.g. confounding variables, inconsistent measures, demand characteristics and investigator effects.

(47) ANSWERS

External (ecological) validity

Q1 Define ecological validity.

Q2 Ebbinghaus's early studies of memory used nonsense syllables. Why do these studies lack ecological validity?

Q3 How is ecological validity related to the issue of generalisability?

Q4 Which are usually more ecologically valid, laboratory or field experiments? Why?

ANSWERS

the extent to which the findings of a study can be applied to different people and situations

A1 The degree to which the findings of a study can be applied to people and situations outside the research situation.

A2 Nonsense syllables are not the kind of material we usually learn, so Ebbinghaus's results might not apply to everyday material.

A3 Generalisability means extending conclusions drawn from research findings to different people and situations; if a study lacks ecological validity, this is not possible.

A4 Field experiments, because they take place in real-life situations, rather than in the artificial situation of a laboratory experiment.

***examiner's* note** Time and culture are issues when considering external (ecological) validity. In replications of the studies of Asch and Milgram, findings have varied considerably across time and in different cultures.

Investigator effects

Q1 Identify two ways in which researchers might interact with participants that could affect responses.

Q2 A change of behaviour in participants aware of being studied is called p............................... r...............................?

Q3 E............................... a............................... may lead to participants adjusting their behaviour because they are concerned that they are being judged.

ANSWERS))

A1 Being friendly; rude; patronising.

A2 participant reactivity

A3 Evaluation apprehension.

***examiner's* note** A further aspect of investigator effects is that researchers come to a study with expectations about the outcome. These expectations could unconsciously bias the researcher in terms of how the procedures of the study are carried out and the results recorded, so that the findings become skewed.

Sample

Q1 Define 'random sample'.

Q2 Milgram advertised in the newspaper for participants for his studies. What kind of a sample was this?

Q3 A student carrying out a piece of research decides to ask co-students to take part. What kind of a sample would this be?

Q4 Why might this sample be biased?

ANSWERS

a group of people who take part in a research study

A1 A sample in which every member of the parent population has an equal chance of being selected to be part of the sample.

A2 A volunteer (self-selecting) sample.

A3 An opportunity sample.

A4 They might only ask students they know personally, so the sample might not be representative of students as a whole. For example, they might only ask people in their year at college, so older/younger students would not be represented.

***examiner's* note** All these sampling methods run the risk of being unrepresentative. However, a larger sample size reduces the likelihood of extreme bias.

Measures of central tendency

Q1 A study measures reaction time (in seconds). Which measure of central tendency would be appropriate, and why?

Q2 Which measure would it be best to use when describing the number of children in the average family?

Q3 Which measure is always a score and is never distorted by an extreme value?

ANSWERS

A1 The mean, as the scores are precise.

A2 The mode.

A3 The mode.

***examiner's* note** The mean is the measure of central tendency generally used with interval (or ratio) level data, the median with ordinal level data, and the mode with nominal level (category) data.

Measures of dispersion

Q1 Scores from a study are: 2 2 3 4 4 6 6 7 8 8 9 18.
What is the interquartile range for these scores?

Q2 For this set of scores, why might the interquartile range be more appropriate than the range?

Q3 A researcher records in seconds how long it takes participants to complete a Stroop list and a similar list of non-colour words. Which measure of dispersion would be most appropriate, and why?

ANSWERS ▶▶

measurement of the spread of a set of scores

A1 The interquartile range is the range of the 50% of scores in the middle. Here this is the range of the central 6 scores, i.e. 8 − 4 = 4.

A2 The range would be distorted by the extreme score of 18.

A3 The standard deviation, since the measurement of time is a precise measurement.

***examiner's* note** Levels of measurement, measures of central tendency and measures of dispersion can be grouped: interval level/mean/standard deviation; ordinal level/median/range (or interquartile range); nominal level/mode/variation ratio.

General adaptation syndrome (GAS)

Q1 What is the main claim made by Selye in his GAS?

Q2 The first part of the response to a stressor prepares the body for f.......... or f........... .

Q3 Selye's research was carried out on rats. In what important way do rats differ from humans, making it advisable to be cautious in generalising his findings to humans?

Q4 Why are the physiological changes associated with the stress response less adaptive now than in our evolutionary past?

ANSWERS

A1 The physiological response to stress is always the same, whatever the nature of the stressor.

A2 fight or flight

A3 Rats do not have the complex cognitions that influence the human response to stress.

A4 Many stressful events cannot be dealt with in physical ways, so there is no outlet for physical responses, which in turn may damage health.

examiner's **note** While there are some problems in generalising Selye's findings directly to humans, his work is useful in suggesting a link between the physiological effects of stress and illness, and could therefore have applications in helping people to cope with stress.

Autonomic nervous system (ANS)

Q1 What are the two divisions of the ANS?

Q2 Which division of the ANS is concerned with the immediate response to stress?

Q3 Is it responsible for self-regulating functions, or those under conscious control? Give an example.

Q4 Which part of the brain is the main control centre for the activities of the ANS?

ANSWERS

A1 Sympathetic and parasympathetic.

A2 Sympathetic.

A3 Self-regulating, such as heart rate and digestion.

A4 The hypothalamus.

***examiner's* note** The sympathetic branch of the ANS is involved in the initial reaction to stress — the alarm reaction in Selye's GAS. In the resistance stage, the parasympathetic branch acts to return the functioning of internal organs, such as the heart, to normal.

Hypothalamic–pituitary–adrenal system

Q1 During the stress response, what does the hormone ACTH (released by the pituitary gland) stimulate?

Q2 This causes c...................... to be released into the bloodstream.

Q3 Identify two effects of these substances.

Q4 What are the implications of these effects?

ANSWERS

A1 Adrenal cortex.

A2 corticosteroids (e.g. cortisol)

A3 Suppresses the immune system; maintains supplies of glucose.

A4 Increases the vulnerability to infection; facilitates a physical response to stress.

examiner's **note** While this describes the general pattern of this aspect of the response to stress, there are variations in the responses of individuals, and to different kinds of situations.

Sympathomedullary pathway

Q1 Which branch of the ANS is involved in this part of the stress response?

Q2 Which part of the adrenal glands is stimulated?

Q3 Which two hormones does this sequence cause to be released into the bloodstream?

Q4 Identify *three* effects of the release of these hormones.

ANSWERS

A1 Sympathetic nervous system (SNS).

A2 Adrenal medulla.

A3 Adrenaline and noradrenaline.

A4 Increased blood pressure; increased heart rate; increased sweat gland activity.

***examiner's* note** This account is limited to the physiological response to stress. How we respond to a stressor will also depend on the psychological appraisal we make of it.

Immune system

Q1 The immune system produces a........................, which remain in the bloodstream and act against returning bacteria or viruses.

Q2 Give two examples of ways in which the immune system may not function well when we are stressed.

Q3 A link has been found between stress and cancer. Why would it be unwise to assume that stress predicts the development of cancer?

Q4 Name a serious disorder other than cancer that has been linked to stress.

ANSWERS

A1 antibodies

A2 Slower healing; higher susceptibility to colds; possible links to headaches.

A3 There are other factors involved, such as an inherited predisposition to develop certain kinds of cancer and exposure to environmental carcinogens such as asbestos.

A4 Hypertension; CHD.

***examiner's* note** In the final (exhaustion) stage of GAS, the immune system is compromised to the extent that resistance to illness is lowered, and what Selye calls 'diseases of adaptation' — such as CHD and hypertension — can occur.

Type A personality

Q1 Identify four characteristics of the Type A personality.

Q2 Which characteristics of the Type A personality are most closely associated with coronary heart disease (CHD)?

Q3 Which researchers proposed the idea of a distinction between Type A and Type B personalities?

Q4 In their research into a possible link between Type A personality and CHD, what was the limitation of the sample?

ANSWERS

personality characterised by competitiveness, hostility and constantly experiencing time pressure

A1 Ambitious; impatient; restless; hostile; angry; competitive; constantly experiencing time pressure.

A2 Anger and hostility.

A3 Friedman & Rosenman.

A4 Only males were included in the sample, so it would not be possible to generalise the findings to females.

examiner's note Research findings in studies investigating a possible link between Type A personality and CHD have been inconsistent. It seems likely that the connection is not entirely straightforward. For example, Williams found that people with Type A personality characteristics had a lower risk of heart disease if they had a positive outlook on life.

Social readjustment rating scale (SRRS)

Q1 What is an LCU?

Q2 According to Holmes & Rahe, what is it about a life event that causes stress?

Q3 Which has the highest LCU value: (a) trouble with the boss; (b) marriage; (c) divorce?

Q4 Studies found that high LCU values are associated with illness. Why does this not prove that a high LCU value causes stress?

ANSWERS

Holmes & Rahe: method of measuring the impact of life events

A1 Life change unit: the numerical value given on the SRRS to a life event reflecting the amount of stress associated with it.

A2 A change, either positive or negative.

A3 (c) divorce — 73; (b) marriage — 53; (a) trouble with the boss — 23.

A4 The studies are correlational, and therefore cannot show cause and effect. It is possible that stress brings about life changes, e.g. illness could lead to trouble with the boss.

***examiner's* note** Life events are often one-off events, so it has been suggested that looking at hassles — everyday small stressors — could provide a more subtle measure of the cumulative effect of more minor stressors. Kanner et al. found that hassles were a better predictor of stress symptoms than LCUs.

Daily hassles

Q1 Which of these events could be described as a hassle: finishing a long-term relationship; forgetting to buy milk; being made redundant from work?

Q2 In what way does the daily hassles approach to stress differ from the life events approach?

Q3 Give one criticism that applies to both the life events and the hassles approach to stress.

Q4 As well as hassles, Kanner also investigated small, pleasant events, such as a friend smiling at you. What did he call this kind of event?

ANSWERS

A1 Forgetting to buy milk.

A2 It looks at small, commonly occurring events rather than at rare, crisis events.

A3 They do not take into account long-term chronic sources of stress; both life events and hassles may be interpreted differently, depending on the person and/or the situation.

A4 An uplift.

examiner's **note** This approach has research support, particularly when hassles and uplifts are considered together, and represents a useful extension to the life events approach, but shares some of its limitations.

Workplace stress

Q1 One source of workplace stress is when people feel they have been given too much work to do, or find their work too difficult. What is this called?

Q2 Identify two other sources of workplace stress.

Q3 Give two examples of jobs that are inevitably stressful.

Q4 Why is work that involves rotating shifts stressful?

ANSWERS

A1 Work overload.

A2 Work underload; role conflict; role strain; changes in the work environment.

A3 Firefighters; paramedics; doctors.

A4 It disrupts circadian rhythms, which must therefore be constantly adapted.

***examiner's* note** Workplace stress is widespread and there is some evidence that it is increasing. Understanding the causes of this kind of stress may help to provide solutions to this kind of problem.

Hardiness

Q1 Define 'commitment' as a factor of the hardy personality.

Q2 Define 'challenge' as a factor of the hardy personality.

Q3 What is the third factor? How can this characteristic be defined?

Q4 Name one factor, other than hardy personality, that might have accounted for the low levels of illness in some executives in highly stressful positions found by Kobasa et al.

ANSWERS

Kobasa: cluster of personality traits, characterised by commitment, challenge and control

A1 Being involved, having a sense of purpose and finding meaning at work and in one's social life.

A2 Potentially stressful events are seen as an opportunity, rather than as a threat.

A3 Control: feeling in control of one's life, and able to influence it.

A4 Social support; exercise.

***examiner's* note** The concept of hardiness has been criticised because: it is difficult to assess; most research in this area has involved middle-class white males; the studies are usually correlational and so cannot show cause and effect. However, it has led to hardiness training, which is an effective treatment for stress.

Emotion-focused coping

Q1 What is the aim of an emotion-focused approach to dealing with stress?

Q2 Emotion-focused coping is also known as p.................... coping.

Q3 Is emotion-focused coping more likely to be used when a person perceives themselves to (a) have some control, or (b) have little control over a stressful situation?

Q4 Which of these is *not* an example of emotion-focused coping used by a student faced with exam stress: trying not to think about the exam; planning answers to possible exam questions; wishing the exam was over?

ANSWERS

A1 To minimise or eliminate the unpleasant emotions associated with stress.

A2 palliative

A3 Little control.

A4 Planning answers to possible exam questions.

examiner's note Emotion-focused coping can be effective in the short term as a way of dealing with stress. It reduces arousal and so makes it easier for the person to develop a more problem-focused approach.

(63) ANSWERS

Problem-focused coping

Q1 What is the aim of a problem-focused approach to dealing with stress?

Q2 Problem-focused coping is also known as i................. coping.

Q3 'In a stressful situation, people tend to use either problem-focused or emotion-focused coping.' True or false?

Q4 Which of these is *not* an example of problem-focused coping used by a student faced with exam stress: reading over class notes; practising answers to possible questions; focusing on events in her life other than the exam?

ANSWERS

A1 To avoid or minimise the threatening situation.

A2 instrumental

A3 False: Folkman and Lazarus found that 98% of their participants used both kinds of coping strategy.

A4 Focusing on events in her life other than the exam.

examiner's **note** People are more likely to use problem-focused coping when they feel they have some control over a situation. It is a less useful approach to stressful situations that are not controllable.

Anxiolytic drugs

Q1 Give two examples of drugs used to treat anxiety.

Q2 Give one advantage of using drugs to treat anxiety.

Q3 Give two possible unwanted effects of their use.

Q4 What is the main limitation of treating someone with drugs to relieve anxiety?

ANSWERS ▶▶

drugs used to treat anxiety

A1 Barbiturates; benzodiazepines (e.g. Librium, Valium); buspirone; beta-blockers.

A2 Patients are likely to respond to drug treatment relatively rapidly; there is a wide choice of drugs available, so it should be possible to find one suitable for a particular patient.

A3 Drugs may be addictive, so withdrawal is a problem; most have side effects, e.g. headaches; some interact with other medication or some foods.

A4 They deal only with the physical symptoms of stress and not its causes.

***examiner's* note** There is no reason why drugs cannot be used in combination with other methods of treatment, e.g. cognitive behavioural methods, to help people avoid future stress, and cope with stress if it occurs again.

Biofeedback

Q1 On which psychological theory is biofeedback based?

Q2 An important part of the treatment is to teach relaxation techniques. Why is this necessary?

Q3 What are the basic principles underlying biofeedback?

Q4 Identify two physiological functions which are usually involved.

ANSWERS

a behavioural method of dealing with stress

A1 Operant conditioning.

A2 Relaxation is used to bring about positive change in physiological functioning.

A3 Patients are given feedback on various physiological functions. They can then learn to control these functions consciously through applying relaxation techniques, and receiving feedback on changes which they have brought about.

A4 Heart rate and blood pressure.

***examiner's* note** Whether biofeedback is the most appropriate method for dealing with stress depends on the person. Some people find it hard to learn the necessary techniques. It is generally successful with children, possibly because they are less sceptical than adults.

Cognitive behavioural approach

Q1 What aspect of this approach does 'cognitive' refer to?

Q2 What two effects should come about if inappropriate thoughts and beliefs are successfully challenged?

Q3 Identify *two* positive aspects of the use of CBT in combating stress.

Q4 Identify *one* limitation in the use of CBT to combat stress.

ANSWERS

an approach to stress management that aims to change inappropriate thinking in order to bring about behaviour change

A1 Challenging inappropriate thoughts and beliefs.

A2 The way we feel about a stressful situation; the action we take in response to it.

A3 Its usefulness has been well supported by research; it can be carried out on a group basis, so is cost-effective; unlike medication, there are no side effects; an individual can apply the basic principles in future stressful situations.

A4 It may not be suitable for someone who is depressed; some people may find it difficult to talk about their problems.

***examiner's* note** While it may not be a suitable way of treating stress for everyone, CBT is an effective way of addressing stress and is widely available, not only face-to-face but through books and computer programs.

Conformity

Q1 How can Jenness's bean study be criticised as a test of conformity?

Q2 In Asch's study, why was the genuine participant last but one to be asked to judge the lines?

Q3 If a person conforms because they want to be accepted as a member of the group, is this compliance or internalisation?

Q4 Identify one factor which may increase resistance to conformity.

ANSWERS

in a group, a change in a person's opinions and/or behaviour as a result of unspoken majority pressure

A1 This was an ambiguous situation. Asch argued that to demonstrate conformity, we should look only at unambiguous situations.

A2 Participants needed to hear a consensus from the majority of the group. It is possible that they were not last in line to reduce demand characteristics.

A3 Compliance — their behaviour has changed but their opinion has not.

A4 Confidence, e.g. from those working in fields where accurate observation is crucial; mentally withdrawing from the group, e.g. by avoiding eye contact.

***examiner's* note** Ethical concerns in this area include deception and stress. However, giving full information at the start would compromise the study. A cost–benefit analysis could be made for this kind of research.

 **ANSWERS**

Normative influence

Q1 If a person responds to normative influence, what is their reason for conforming?

Q2 Identify an alternative kind of influence.

Q3 If a person responds to this kind of influence, what is their reason for conforming?

Q4 In an unambiguous situation, as in the Asch line study, which kind of influence is more likely?

ANSWERS

A1 A need to be accepted by the group.

A2 Informational.

A3 A need to be right.

A4 Normative influence.

***examiner's* note** The relative strengths of the kinds of influence will depend on the individual and the situation. Some studies, e.g. Insko et al., have found that normative and informational influence can work in combination to increase conformity.

Internalisation

Q1 What is the difference between internalisation and compliance?

Q2 Does internalisation relate to normative or informational influence?

Q3 Is internalisation more likely in an ambiguous or an unambiguous situation?

Q4 Is internalisation more likely when the individual feels competent to make a judgement, or when they are uncertain?

ANSWERS

A1 Compliance involves a change of behaviour but not of opinion; internalisation involves a change in both opinion and behaviour.

A2 Informational influence.

A3 In an ambiguous situation.

A4 In a situation where a person feels uncertain.

***examiner's* note** When people are put into an ambiguous situation, they are more likely to refer to others to see how they should respond. Festinger calls this 'social comparison'. It is in these circumstances that internalisation — involving a change of opinion — is most likely.

Social roles

Q1 Give two examples of behaviours associated with the role of 'student'.

Q2 How is the idea of social roles linked to Zimbardo's prison experiment?

Q3 In Zimbardo's study, which major factor — other than being allocated the role of prisoner or guard — did Zimbardo suggest promoted behaviour in line with these roles?

ANSWERS ▶▶

A1 Attending classes; writing essays; doing homework; reading relevant materials.

A2 Being allocated the role of prisoner or guard triggered behaviours considered typical of the role.

A3 The realistic prison setting.

***examiner's* note** In Zimbardo's study, the screening of potential participants, together with random allocation as prisoners or guards, supports the idea that the behaviour shown by participants was the result of adopting roles rather than individual differences. The demonstration in this study of the influence of an institutional setting on social roles was positive in leading to some reform of the prison system in the USA.

Protection from harm

Q1 BPS guidelines state that participants should be protected from any physical/psychological harm greater than ....
....

Q2 In Milgram's study, what psychological harm might participants have experienced?

Q3 How did Milgram defend himself against the claim that he had caused his participants psychological harm?

ANSWERS

A1 …that experienced in everyday life.

A2 Participants realised they had given painful shocks to a middle-aged man with a heart condition when instructed to do so by someone with no real authority over them. It is likely to have affected their self-esteem.

A3 He claimed they had caused themselves harm by choosing to obey the instructions. He pointed out that it is not the job of psychologists to protect people from self-knowledge.

***examiner's* note** The guidelines in this area go beyond protection from harm. They say that participants should be assured that personal questions need not be answered and should be reassured of confidentiality and anonymity.

Obedience

Q1 In Milgram's study, what percentage of participants obeyed the order to give shocks to the upper limit of 450 volts?

Q2 What reduced this obedience level more effectively: (a) the study being carried out in an office; (b) a disobedient model?

Q3 It is claimed that this study lacked experimental realism. Give one point supporting this idea, and one point contradicting it.

Q4 How did Meeus & Raaijmakers extend this research?

ANSWERS

A1 65%.

A2 (b) obedience was 10%; (a) only reduced obedience levels to 47.5%.

A3 Support: there was no reason why the experimenter could not have administered the shocks; the participants might not have believed that real shocks were given. Contradiction: a sample shock suggested that genuine shocks were given.

A4 Meeus & Raaijmakers showed that people will follow orders to inflict psychological harm, not only physical harm.

examiner's note Levels of obedience have been shown to vary between individuals, with gender and across cultures, though findings have not always been consistent. Any differences found may be the result of procedural variation.

Foot-in-the-door technique

Q1 What is the foot-in-the-door technique?

Q2 If you wanted to borrow £20, how would you apply this technique to improve your chances of getting the money?

Q3 Which aspect of Milgram's study suggests that this contributed to the high levels of participant obedience?

Q4 Which aspects of Milgram's study suggest that this is not a complete explanation for the high levels of obedience?

ANSWERS

a way of achieving compliance by gradually increasing the requests made

A1 Making a small request, making a larger request if the first is successful, and continuing to increase the request until the target is achieved.

A2 Ask to borrow £5. If that is agreed, ask whether they could make it £10. If yes, say that £20 would be better, to be on the safe side.

A3 The shocks started at 15 volts, and increased in 15-volt intervals. Each small increment would not produce a noticeably more painful shock.

A4 Participants could not believe that the shocks were still mild when Mr Wallace was apparently screaming in pain, yet 65% continued to give shocks.

examiner's note Some obedience studies cannot be explained by this technique. In Hofling's study of nurses, the idea of an agentic state seems more useful.

Agentic state

Q1 What is meant by Milgram's term 'agentic state'?

Q2 How does it contrast with an autonomous state?

Q3 Which aspects of Milgram's experiments would have encouraged a shift to an agentic state?

Q4 What happened in Milgram's study when orders were given via a tape recording, rather than in person? How might this be linked to the idea of an agentic state?

ANSWERS

A1 A cognitive state in which we act on behalf of another person.

A2 In an autonomous state (unlike an agentic state), we are aware of the consequences of our actions and accept responsibility for them.

A3 The experimenter was presented as an authority figure; the experimenter explicitly stated that he accepted full responsibility for anything which happened in the course of the study.

A4 Obedience dropped markedly to 20%. An agentic state is less likely to occur in the physical absence of the authority figure.

examiner's note Milgram suggested that the agentic state was an evolutionary development, facilitating the functioning of social systems. It would be difficult for hierarchical social groups to function effectively if lower-ranking individuals did not readily obey those higher up.

Authoritarian personality

Q1 Who developed the concept of the authoritarian personality?

Q2 What are the key characteristics of this personality type?

Q3 How is this personality type measured?

Q4 Why is the authoritarian personality type so willing to obey orders?

ANSWERS

A1 Adorno.

A2 Conventionality; submission to those in authority; aggression towards those of lower rank; superstition; prejudice.

A3 The F-Scale.

A4 Adorno et al. often found that people with these traits had parents who expected unquestioning obedience and punished disobedience severely. In later life, authority figures (symbolising the parent) are responded to as the child did to the parent.

***examiner's* note** There are other factors which lead to individual differences in the extent to which people obey orders. A key factor seems to be experience. One of Milgram's participants, who had grown up in Nazi Germany, refused to give shocks above 210 volts, saying: 'Perhaps we have seen too much pain.'

Cost–benefit analysis

Q1 What is the aim of a cost–benefit analysis?

Q2 How would a cost–benefit analysis be carried out?

Q3 Give two costs and two benefits of Milgram's study.

Q4 Give two costs and two benefits of Zimbardo's study.

ANSWERS

A1 To evaluate a study by weighing up positive and negative aspects.

A2 Identify the positive and negative aspects, and give each a weighting in terms of its importance, to make a comparison of the two sides.

A3 Costs: deception; stress; loss of self-esteem. Benefits: gave unexpected information about obedience; triggered further research.

A4 Costs: incomplete information given to participants about procedures; extreme stress; loss of self-esteem. Benefits: gave information about power relationships; triggered research into shyness; changes made to US prison system.

***examiner's* note** In practice, cost–benefit analyses are difficult to carry out. It is often hard to predict what the costs of a study will be, and judgements are subjective. However, this kind of analysis may provide a rough way of evaluating a study.

(77) ANSWERS

Independent behaviour

Q1 Give an example of one of the variations of Milgram's study in which participants were much more likely to show independent behaviour than in the original experiment.

Q2 Give an example of one personal characteristic associated with more independent behaviour in conformity studies.

Q3 In Asch's study of conformity, the percentage of participants who showed consistently independent behaviour was:

(a) 32%   (b) 25%   (c) 12%

ANSWERS

A1 Absence of the experimenter; learner in the same room.

A2 Confidence; extraversion; higher level of education; having an
internal locus of control.

A3 (b) 25%.

***examiner's* note** A positive aspect of studies of social influence is that the
investigation of characteristics associated with independent behaviour may
suggest ways in which people can be encouraged to resist conformity where
this is inappropriate, e.g. assertiveness training in reducing substance abuse in
young people through conformity to peers, and alerting them to the dangers of
accepting unquestioningly orders given by an authority figure.

Locus of control

Q1 People who believe that events come about largely through their own actions and efforts have a high .... locus of control.

Q2 People who believe that events come about largely due to the actions of other people, chance or luck have a high .... locus of control.

Q3 Give one way in which someone with a high external locus of control might explain doing badly in an exam.

Q4 Which kind of person might be expected to be more likely to conform to the judgements of others, someone with a high external or a high internal locus of control?

ANSWERS

A1 internal

A2 external

A3 The questions were unfair; they were badly taught; they were ill
on the day of the exam; they were unlucky with the questions.

A4 External.

examiner's note Rotter's concept of locus of control has been shown to be
useful in terms of individual differences in social influence research. However,
the evidence is relatively weak, and individual differences in this area are likely
to interact with situational factors.

Individualist culture

Q1 What is meant by the description of a culture as individualist?

Q2 Identify and outline the features of the kind of culture with which it is contrasted.

Q3 In which of these two kinds of culture might social influence be expected to be stronger?

Q4 Identify *one* limitation of the individualist/collectivist distinction.

ANSWERS ▶▶

A1 A culture in which the emphasis is on the rights and responsibilities of the individual.

A2 Collectivist culture, in which the emphasis is on the needs and expectations of the social group.

A3 Collectivist.

A4 Within a culture, there may be important differences between sub-cultures; cultures are not static but change over time, e.g. as a result of sociopolitical factors.

***examiner's* note** While the individualist/collectivist distinction may be an oversimplification, it has nonetheless been shown to be a useful way of examining broad cultural factors in social influence research.

Deviation from social norms

Q1 The implicit behavioural expectations of a social group which are violated in this definition of abnormality are called r............... rules.

Q2 Who is the main critic of the criterion of 'deviation from social norms', suggesting it is a way of controlling people of whom society disapproves?

Q3 Why can this criterion for defining people as abnormal not differentiate clearly between normal and abnormal?

Q4 Identify *one* issue with this definition other than the difficulty of making a clear distinction between normal and abnormal.

ANSWERS

A1 residual

A2 Szasz.

A3 It relies on a subjective interpretation of behaviour, so different individuals are likely to differ in how the criterion is applied.

A4 Behaviour must be judged in relation to the situation within which it takes place; it may be legitimate to fail to observe some social norms, e.g. racist attitudes.

***examiner's* note** This definition of abnormality can be useful as part of an assessment, but one difficulty is that norms vary across time, e.g. homosexuality was regarded as a disorder 30 years ago, but is now generally regarded as falling within social norms.

Failure to function adequately

Q1 What term describes behaviour suggesting failure to function adequately?

Q2 Personal distress is an example of a failure to function adequately. What is the problem with using this criterion?

Q3 'Failure to function adequately' includes bizarre behaviour. Give an example of a disorder meeting this criterion.

Q4 Identify *two* other ways in which behaviour may demonstrate failure to function adequately.

ANSWERS

behaviour which does not allow the individual to function as an individual and in a social group

A1 Maladaptive.

A2 In some circumstances, e.g. bereavement, personal distress would be seen as a normal response.

A3 Holding a conversation with voices in your head, often found in schizophrenia; obsessive hand-washing, a common characteristic of OCD.

A4 Causing distress to others; behaving unpredictably.

examiner's note None of the attempts to define abnormality is entirely adequate, as they often involve subjective judgements. For this reason, Rosenhan & Seligman suggested that combining the criteria proposed by these definitions might provide a better way of deciding whether a person's behaviour could be defined as abnormal.

Biological (medical) model

Q1 This model assumes that the causes of mental disorders are physical, and so are referred to as mental i..................... .

Q2 For which of these disorders is there good evidence of genetic factors: (a) phobia; (b) depression; (c) schizophrenia?

Q3 Identify *two* possible causes of mental disorder, other than genes, proposed by this model.

Q4 Using this model, how are mental disorders treated?

ANSWERS

A1 illness

A2 (c) schizophrenia.

A3 Brain damage; biochemical malfunction (hormones, neurotransmitters).

A4 They should be treated using physical methods, i.e. drugs, ECT or psychosurgery.

examiner's note One positive aspect of this model is that the individual cannot be blamed for their disorder. However, while labelling someone with a mental illness removes blame, it can also lead to prejudice and discrimination.

Neurotransmitters

Q1 Neurotransmitters are known as chemical m............................
because they carry information between neurons.

Q2 Most research in this area looks for a link between an
imbalance of neurotransmitters and mental illness. What
is the drawback of this method?

Q3 Which is the main neurotransmitter associated with
depression?

Q4 Which neurotransmitter is associated with schizophrenia?

ANSWERS

A1 messengers

A2 It cannot show that the imbalance of neurotransmitters causes
the disorders. It could be that the disorder causes the imbalance
of neurotransmitters.

A3 Serotonin.

A4 Dopamine.

***examiner's* note** Mental illness can be associated with either too much of a
particular neurotransmitter (e.g. the link between dopamine and schizophrenia)
or too little (e.g. the link between serotonin and depression).

Hormones

Q1 What are hormones?

Q2 Which pituitary hormone is associated with the stress response?

Q3 Which two hormones are associated with changes in heart rate, sweat gland activity and blood pressure during the stress response?

Q4 Disorders of which gland have been linked to depression?

ANSWERS

A1 Chemicals released by the glands making up the endocrine system.

A2 ACTH.

A3 Adrenaline and noradrenaline.

A4 The thyroid.

***examiner's* note** It is often difficult to establish cause-and-effect relationships between hormone levels and mental disorders. Hormones can be influenced by emotional factors, so any link between a hormone imbalance and a mental disorder could be indirect.

Psychodynamic model

Q1 Identify *three* factors proposed by this model to be involved in the development of mental disorder.

Q2 Using this model, what is the appropriate treatment for mental health problems? What is the aim of the therapy?

Q3 Give one strength of this model.

Q4 Freud saw eating as symbolic of sexual expression. How could this explain the development of anorexia nervosa?

ANSWERS

A1 Psychic conflict; defence mechanisms; psychosexual fixation.

A2 Psychoanalysis — to bring unconscious material into consciousness so that it can be dealt with.

A3 It removes blame from the person with a mental disorder; the treatment aims to uncover the causes, so improvement should be permanent.

A4 Failure to eat could be a way of keeping the body in a childlike state, avoiding adult sexuality or the responsibility which being an adult brings.

examiner's note There is some support for the idea that childhood experiences play a role in adult mental disorders. For example, abuse in childhood is almost invariably linked with adult mental health problems. However, Freud's ideas are difficult if not impossible to test objectively.

Defence mechanisms

Q1 What is the function of defence mechanisms?

Q2 Repression is one example of a defence mechanism.
How can it be defined?

Q3 What is the disadvantage of a defence mechanism such as repression?

Q4 Which defence mechanism is an effective way of expressing unconscious material?

ANSWERS

A1 They protect us from anxiety by holding threatening material in the unconscious.

A2 Motivated forgetting — material is pushed into the unconscious so that we are no longer aware of it.

A3 The material is still in the unconscious, and so can continue to affect us.

A4 Sublimation.

***examiner's* note** Defence mechanisms are unconscious ways of preventing traumatic material, usually from childhood, from reaching consciousness. However, apart from sublimation, they are only effective in the short term. In the long term, psychoanalysis is necessary to deal effectively with such problems.

Psychic conflict

Q1 What are the three parts of the mind that may be in conflict, leading to mental disorders?

Q2 In the mentally healthy person, which part of the mind is in control?

Q3 In a psychopath, which part of the mind is in control?

Q4 What are the characteristics of a person with an extremely strong superego?

ANSWERS

A1 Id, ego and superego.

A2 Ego.

A3 Id.

A4 Neurotic anxiety, because there will be an exaggerated focus on what the person ought to do (ego ideal) and ought not to do (conscience).

***examiner's* note** Psychic conflict is just one element in the psychodynamic explanation of mental disorders. Traumatic experiences in childhood, which have usually been repressed, and fixation in one of the psychosexual stages also have a role to play.

Classical conditioning

Q1 Within the behaviourist perspective, classical conditioning sees mental disorders as l................ m.................... b................ .

Q2 In this theory, learning takes place through an association being formed between a s........................ and a r........................

Q3 In which study did Watson & Rayner first demonstrate classical conditioning in a human?

Q4 In this study, which mental disorder was created?

ANSWERS

A1 learned maladaptive behaviour

A2 stimulus; response

A3 'Little Albert'.

A4 A phobia of a white rat.

***examiner's* note** The 'Little Albert' study shows that phobias can be learned, but it does not follow that all phobias are necessarily learned in this way.

Some disorders are hard to explain in terms of learning, particularly where there seems to be a strong genetic element, e.g. schizophrenia.

Operant conditioning

Q1 What is the association formed in operant conditioning?

Q2 The theory proposes that maladaptive behaviour can be r........................, e.g. by attention from parents.

Q3 In this model, what is the basic principle on which therapy is based?

Q4 In operant conditioning, how might restricting food intake be thought to lead to anorexia nervosa?

ANSWERS

A1 An association between behaviour and its consequences.

A2 reinforced

A3 Since the behaviour has been learned, it can be unlearned, and more adaptive behaviour learned in its place.

A4 Losing weight could be reinforced by praise from others. It could become a habit, and then be further reinforced by attention when others voice concern about excessive weight loss.

***examiner's* note** In both classical and operant conditioning, the behaviour is the problem, and the cause of the problem is seen as irrelevant, so the aim of therapy is to cause behaviour change. One way in which this is done using operant conditioning techniques is a token economy, where people are given tokens for appropriate behaviour, which can later be exchanged for reinforcers of their choosing.

Social learning theory (SLT)

Q1 Name the theorist most closely associated with SLT.

Q2 SLT claims that we learn from the outcome of others' behaviour, rather than our own. This is v............................ conditioning.

Q3 Name the terms for learning behaviour through observing others, and for adopting their behaviour.

Q4 In this theory, what are the three sources of information from which we learn behaviour?

ANSWERS

A1 Bandura.

A2 vicarious

A3 Observational learning; modelling.

A4 The family; the sub-culture; the media.

***examiner's* note** There is strong evidence for a link between eating disorders and the media. Through the media, young women learn the cultural norm that slim equals good, and that dieting is normal. This would help to account for the prevalence of eating disorders in Western countries, while they are almost unknown in some other cultures, such as China.

Biological preparedness

Q1 Which theorist is associated with the concept of biological preparedness?

Q2 Seligman claimed that some phobias are very common because they were a..................... in our evolutionary past.

Q3 Explain what is meant by 'adaptive' in this context.

Q4 Give *three* examples of phobias that could be explained in this way, and explain why they would be adaptive.

ANSWERS

A1 Seligman.

A2 adaptive

A3 Phobias would promote survival long enough to reproduce and pass on genes to the next generation, including the genes that code for the phobia.

A4 Heights: avoiding danger of falling; spiders and snakes: avoiding potentially being poisoned; enclosed spaces (claustrophobia): avoiding suffocation and limitations to possible responses in dangerous situations; water: avoiding danger of drowning.

***examiner's* note** There is some research support for this idea. For example, Mineka and Cook found that it was easier to create in monkeys a phobia of a snake than a flower. However, genetic factors and vicarious learning also appear to be important in the development of phobias.

Cognitive model

Q1 What does this model suggest is the cause of mental disorders?

Q2 How does this model suggest disorders should be treated?

Q3 Give one example of this kind of treatment.

Q4 What are the three areas of Beck's negative triad?

ANSWERS

A1 The person has developed maladaptive ways of thinking.

A2 These ways of thinking need to be challenged and changed.

A3 Cognitive behavioural therapy (CBT); rational emotive behaviour therapy (REBT).

A4 Inappropriate thoughts of self, circumstances and the future.

***examiner's* note** There is strong evidence of distorted thinking in anorexia nervosa and bulimia nervosa, since in both disorders sufferers have a distorted body image, seeing themselves as fatter than they actually are. However, it is not clear whether this is the cause or the result of the disorder.

The diathesis–stress model

Q1 What is the basic idea behind this model?

Q2 What could create the predisposition suggested by the term 'diathesis'?

Q3 Given that the typical age of onset of anorexia nervosa is early to mid-teens, what kinds of stressors could trigger its development?

Q4 How does this model bring together 'nature' and 'nurture' views about the development of mental disorders?

ANSWERS

individuals may have a predisposition to develop a disorder, triggered by environmental stress

A1 People may have a predisposition to develop a mental disorder, but will only go on to develop it if it is triggered by stressful experiences.

A2 It could be genetic or the result of early experience, e.g. losing a parent in childhood might predispose to depression in later life.

A3 For females, the start of periods could be a trigger, symbolic of the move from child to adult; concerns about first romantic relationships; exam stress.

A4 Interaction between a predisposing factor, usually genetic (nature), and stress in the environment (nurture).

examiner's note This model is useful in helping to explain the development of disorders where there is a strong genetic link (e.g. schizophrenia), but not everyone with a genetic predisposition develops it.

Chemotherapy

Q1 Identify the four main groups of drugs used to treat mental illness.

Q2 Some anti-anxiety drugs can be addictive. Why is this a problem when the patient stops taking them?

Q3 Identify one ethical issue with the use of drugs to treat mental illness.

Q4 How might the exclusive use of drugs to treat mental illness be seen to be limited?

ANSWERS

A1 Anxiolytics (minor tranquillisers); stimulants; antidepressants; antipsychotics (major tranquillisers).

A2 The patient is likely to experience unpleasant withdrawal symptoms.

A3 A patient can be sectioned and given drugs against his or her will.

A4 There may well be other factors — psychological and social — that contribute to the illness and that are not addressed by the use of drugs.

***examiner's* note** While drugs may offer only limited treatment for some illnesses, they can nonetheless be very helpful and also be used alongside other psychological interventions as part of the effective treatment of mental illness.

Antipsychotics (major tranquillisers)

Q1 Which *two* neurotransmitters are affected by modern antipsychotic drugs?

Q2 A relatively rare but potentially serious side effect of traditional antipsychotics is t.................. d........................, resulting in jerky movements of the face, mouth and sometimes limbs.

Q3 As a result of problems with traditional antipsychotic drugs, a new generation of drugs has been developed, known as a................... antipsychotics.

Q4 For which kinds of symptoms of schizophrenia, positive or negative, are antipsychotics generally more effective?

ANSWERS

A1 Dopamine and serotonin.

A2 tardive dyskinesia

A3 atypical

A4 Positive.

***examiner's* note** As with all drugs, antipsychotics have potential side effects. These possible costs need to be weighed against the possible benefits of their use, in terms of allowing people with a psychotic illness to lead relatively normal lives.

Electroconvulsive therapy (ECT)

Q1 For which disorder is ECT mainly used?

Q2 It has been suggested that ECT may be effective as it acts as a placebo. What is meant by this?

Q3 Which is more effective, unilateral or bilateral ECT?

Q4 ECT usually causes some memory loss in the patient for the period leading up to the treatment. This is called r................... amnesia.

ANSWERS

A1 Depression.

A2 It is effective because patients expect it to be effective.

A3 Bilateral.

A4 retrograde

***examiner's* note** There are issues with the use of ECT, including incomplete understanding of how it works, memory loss, brain damage and the ethics of using it for patients under section. However, for severely depressed and often suicidal patients, the costs may be outweighed by the benefits of successful treatment.

Psychoanalysis

Q1 What is the aim of psychoanalysis?

Q2 Identify the main technique used, where patients are encouraged to talk about whatever comes into their minds.

Q3 In dream analysis, the m............... content (the story and images of the dream) is interpreted in terms of its l................... content (its symbolic meaning).

Q4 It has been suggested that the kind of deep analysis used in this therapy can lead to patients 'remembering' events that may never have happened. What is this called?

ANSWERS

A1 To bring unconscious material into consciousness so that it can be 'worked through'.

A2 Free association.

A3 manifest; latent

A4 False memory syndrome.

examiner's note Psychoanalysis has been criticised for its emphasis on interpretation by the analyst and the difficulty of establishing its effectiveness. It is also time-consuming and therefore expensive, and may not be suitable for every patient. However, it involves establishing and dealing with the causes of problems, which should therefore not recur when analysis is completed.

Systematic desensitisation

Q1 What is a hierarchy of fear?

Q2 Why is a person who is being treated using this method taught relaxation techniques?

Q3 One variation of the therapy is vicarious desensitisation, where models showing or learning appropriate behaviours are used. On which theory is this based?

Q4 Identify one positive and one negative aspect of this therapy.

ANSWERS

A1 Description of a set of situations from the least threatening to one that causes maximum anxiety.

A2 So that they can consciously relax as they move through the stages of the hierarchy of fear.

A3 Social learning theory (SLT).

A4 Positive: can be used with anyone; quick and therefore cheap; can be combined with other therapies. Negative: does not address causes; limited in the kinds of disorders for which it can be used; stimulus substitution may occur; the effects may not be generalisable.

***examiner's* note** Systematic desensitisation has been criticised on ethical grounds, in terms of the therapist's control over the patient. However, ideally the patient should take control of when he or she is ready to move to the next stage of the hierarchy of fear.

(99) ANSWERS

Cognitive behavioural therapy (CBT)

Q1 Who developed REBT (rational-emotive behaviour therapy), the original form of CBT?

Q2 Ellis developed the ABC model: a.................... event; b............. about (a); c........................ of (b), in terms of feelings and behaviour.

Q3 What is meant in CBT by 'homework'?

Q4 For which kinds of disorders does CBT not appear to have much to offer?

ANSWERS

therapy that involves modifying inappropriate
thinking and so bringing about behaviour change

A1 Albert Ellis.

A2 activating; beliefs; consequences

A3 Asking patients to act against their irrational beliefs to discover
for themselves that there are no appalling consequences.

A4 Psychotic, such as schizophrenia.

examiner's note CBT has been found to be effective in treating a range of
disorders, including depression, phobias and other anxiety disorders such as
OCD, and eating disorders. It also has the advantage of providing patients with
self-help techniques that they can use if problems arise in the future.